Resting in the Familiar

RESTING IN THE FAMILIAR

CHRISTINE M. KENDALL

Originally Published by
Independent Writers' Studio Press

ISBN: 978-0-9975453-5-7

Methow Press
P.O. Box 1213
Twisp, WA 98856

To all those who have encouraged me, especially Jack Kienast.

Contents

ABOUT THE AUTHOR

Aunt Kaye sat at her kitchen table in Burien, Washington, her legs crossed. She wore a worn white robe; a cup of coffee steaming in front of her as she began to read aloud from a slim book, *The Pill Versus the Springhill Mine Disaster.*

Listening to her, I was entranced and set free to write poetry, like my dad, like my grandmother before him, but at the same time not like them at all.

Sometimes I imagine Aunt Kaye and my muse sitting together discovering new poetry, taking turns saying: *Listen to this one,* their heads nodding in agreement over some poems, eyebrows raised over others. I think of the day my aunt Kaye passed away and how I felt her spirit rush past me and her whispering in my ear: *This is your time.* That was a while back, but hearkening to it now I feel this is the time to put out a second collection of poetry.

I thank Mary Elizabeth Gillilan, Norman L. Green and my partner Jack for their support in this endeavor.

PART 1

RESTING IN THE FAMILIAR

EARLY MORNING

. . . and the poets are at their window
—Billy Collins

Turkey Vultures circle lower and lower above
Little Squalicum Beach—something putrid
attracts them—with binoculars I see their red,
wrinkly masks, their solemn, mournful faces.

Their wingtip feathers spread and curl, their size
amazes, accustomed as I am to seagulls, crows,
and, hummingbirds who hover outside my kitchen window
to sip blooms of red hot poker.

These tiny birds astonish in darting territorial battles, thrust
needle-like beaks against their fellows. Turkey Vultures
appear docile; their languid flight uses thermals and slight
alterations in attitude for descents with barely a flap of wings.

So it is most mornings we poets stand looking out
our windows, cups of coffee or tea in hand to survey
our surroundings—starting our days as Billy Collins says
we do—watching the day unfold and begin to write itself.

Fragment of poem written and note by Nelle (McLeod) Anderson Brown Johansen (1896-1966) in Fishtown on the Skagit River

THE FRAGMENT

You start to fish as day is done
and don't pick up 'till rising sun
If fish keep coming all the season
a stake I'll make or know the reason.

THE NOTE

Some guys up at La Conner say Clarence didn't catch those 37 Tyees but got them from non-union fishermen. It's a <u>damn</u> lie as I saw him catch them all. <u>Sour Grapes</u> is all it is.

MY GRANDMA NELLE

My grandma Nelle lived in Fishtown when fishermen lived there,
long before the hippies and artists moved in to make it their place.
My grandma Nelle was a story teller, she made them up—
wrote poetry, played piano, lived simply, so she could clean her house
in an hour or less. She needed time for her writing,
including letters to friends; and in Fishtown on the Skagit,
long after Simon drowned, she lived with Clarence, an Indian man,
but it was short-lived.

Clarence had a rocking chair which would *creak, creak, creak,*

when he was home rocking—not one to be still—

and the noise drove Nelle crazy, along with living out there

in the boonies where all the talk was about fish—catching them,

not catching them, almost catching them, and eating them

morning, noon, and night.

One day when Nelle's man was off fishing, in a fit of had-it-

up-to-here with a little vengeance thrown in, she sawed

the rockers off his chair, walked out of Fishtown

and that was that.

THANKSGIVING

The conversation at the big table
is full and rich as Aunt Cissy's
chiffon cream pumpkin pie.

The baby bangs her spoon
on her highchair tray, gurgles,
smiles wide when all eyes
are upon her, until conversation
resumes and the noise of knives,
forks, and clink of china, smack of
lips, scrape of serving spoons fills
the air along with all the talk:

Uncle Arnold has the floor
even though Aunt Edie tries and
tries to get her two cents in about
old friends, family trees, and how
they branch and intertwine.

It's difficult to follow.
Great Aunt Louise does not need
to try, she is too busy as her hand
delivers food to her mouth in slow
shaky movements; she occasionally

pauses to look around the table—
shyly, with a sweet smile.

Her head swims with all this talk,
plus the perfumes these girls wear,
the abundance of foodstuff, the gleam
of silver, crystal, and damask linen in
candlelight.

Memories take her away, she returns
to Indiana in the 1920s,
Uncle Otto carving *The Bird*, it is always
The Bird, as if it is the only one. He serves it
up, white meat to Hattie, dark for Uncle Mel.

Aunt Louise returns to the present,
startled, as if among strangers, twists
the napkin in her lap, adjusts to this
situation, so many new faces, so many
faces missing. She and the baby
the ends of the family spectrum.
She decides to make a toast:

To my 96th Thanksgiving and finest
one ever, thank you.

Great Aunt Louise has spoken.

SCYTHES AND BROOMS

I watched my father scything
at my great aunt Esther's place,
cutting through the field, taking down
hay in sweeping, rhythmic movements
side-to-side starting at the periphery.

He worked around that tall grass field
until it was laid down and there was hay
to rake into piles, work done so quietly
you could still hear birdsong.

I think of that when I sweep outside,
the broom makes whisk-whisk-whisking
noises as I brush debris into small piles
swept with short strokes into a dustpan.

I like my tools with wooden handles,
without batteries or gas motors,
there's satisfaction in using my muscles
and being aware of nature's sounds.

FAMILY STORIES

Retold many times can be so comfortable
you sink into them like sitting on a couch
with plump pillows, resting in the familiar
with an expectation of what comes next—
knowing when to laugh, when to chime in
with your telling of what took place—
a story well-varnished by re-tellings.

There is for instance my family's story
of traveling across the country in 1959,
my brother Shaun—eight years old—quiet, bookish,
the youngest, spoke up with startling authority.
We had passed billboard after enticing billboard,
with brightly painted words that read:
Prehistoric Monsters, Visit the Petrified Forest,
Pet a Two-Headed Calf. Billboards that made
your head swivel. Shaun begged my dad to stop
at these wonders of the world that blossomed
out of barren landscapes like promising oases.

My older brother Simon and I were amused—
we knew you couldn't slow down a fighter pilot
accustomed to travel at supersonic speeds;
we'd been reminded that if he were flying a plane

we'd be there by now. We stopped on trips only
for essentials: late breakfasts after early starts,
gasoline when necessary, restrooms a pit stop
and we had to be fast, no lollygagging allowed.

After seeing a series of signs for Goat's Milk Fudge,
Shaun made fresh pleas to stop, but Dad
kept driving, so Shaun quietly announced with
crisp words: *When you're an old man and I'm driving,
if you see something you want me to stop for, I won't stop.*

The brakes came on so quickly, so hard and fast,
we were all thrust forward. The fighter pilot stopped,
backed up, parked the car, got out, strode to the stand
taking dollars out of his billfold and bought the goat's milk
fudge so sickeningly sweet on our empty stomachs
none of us can recommend it to this day.

Fish Tale

Summers of my youth in Washington State
were spent on islands: Whidbey and Camano,
where my parents, aunts and uncles fished
for salmon relentlessly.

Up before dawn they went out in wooden boats
with slatted seats and an outboard motor,
spoons to lure a fighting king salmon polished
to a high shine.

They didn't have VHF radios, electronic
fish finders, or down riggers. They knew
the hot spots and there were fish to catch.
They took a little lunch, a thermos of tea
for my mom, a few cold beers for my dad,
fished until they caught their limit—if not,
returned at dusk.

I learned early on fishing was not for me.
Once out in the boat trolling back and forth,
and back and forth, my patience and imagination
had limits, my time was spent in envied wonder
at the doings of my cousins playing on the beach,

or in the in fields or woods while I was hostage
to my own desire to go out in the boat.

I failed to understand the lure of this passion—
even if the worst thing happened and someone
had a strike. The arc of the pole, zinging run
of the fish line, all other lines quickly reeled in,
shouts of: *Check the drag, let it play, reel 'em in close
to the boat, grab the gaff hook, get the dip net,* filled the air.

If in all this melee the gleaming silver salmon was caught,
so was I, seeing it laid out in a box beneath the middle seat,
some scales lost, sticking like sequins wherever they fell,
the bright round eye of the salmon staring, I thought
pleading to be saved, mouth slowly opening and closing,
gills working their last, blood splattered here and there—

Summers of my youth I learned early on fishing was not for me.

Fish In Our Albums

In my family's photo albums
there are pictures of fish—
we weren't catch and release people.
Fish were for the frying pan,
for the freezer, for canning,
fish were for eating for God's sake,
usually the fresher the better.

In the photographs my dad, uncles,
aunts, even my mother hold king salmon,
huge ones hefted high and proudly so.
The fish are bigger than the children
who somehow inched into the photo
sessions with silly grins.

There are halibuts being hugged,
man-sized fish difficult to bring on
board. Stories are told about those
episodes you wouldn't want to hear.
There are trout on strings so long
you wonder how that many fish
could be caught, let alone eaten.

The deckle-edged black and white
photos capture family reunions,
fish on platters to feast upon,
baked or smoked, possibly fried.
It's easy to see fishing was the
family's passion, and those photos
of fish are as familiar as relatives.

BELLINGHAM TO NELLIS AFB

On the road to Nevada, Simon, six years old,

navigated the way Great Uncle Charlie taught him

at his kitchen table in Tacoma, our first stop on our trip.

Simon sat in the front seat, map on his lap, took his job

seriously, watched for road signs, traced the journey, a finger

kept place while he guided our mother, a novice driver

who had never driven far.

Our second night we stayed near Mt. Hood, huge icicles

hung outside windows like fangs of a giant beast; we studied

them from the warmth of the inn. Traveling on, snow, ice,

evergreens, and grey skies disappeared, we entered an arid

landscape, our apple-red cheeks branded us outsiders unlike

well-tanned Nevadans.

The landmark used to find Nellis was a tall red and white

checkered water tower. With crayons Simon carefully drew

a picture of the base: the checkered tower, jet planes, the beige

two-story barracks we lived in while our dad was a student

at Fighter Weapons Training before shipping out for Korea.

Little did I know then we were military kids, checkered water towers were a familiar landmark of home wherever we went. Today whenever I see them I feel an old uprooted sensation, but on the road to Nevada sitting in the backseat I had no idea of roads we would travel or the places we would call home.

FIRST BICYCLE, NELLIS AFB

It took only two revolutions and I knew
I had both training wheels off the ground.
I was balanced and airborne and free. I zoomed
down Wright Street named for the famous
brothers who made flight possible.

You'd think my own pilot father would have
been proud of me and taken those wheels off
pronto when I asked every night at dinner.
But no, it was the 1950s and maybe he was
coddling me, or just too busy to remove them.

So friends helped me. We wrenched the shameful baby
wheels off, and fortune shone, as their mother
backed down her driveway and flattened them
good. Freed of them I spoke up at dinner of their
removal and damages beyond repair.

MILITARY BRATS

First of all, most of us weren't brats,
not in the usual sense of the word.

Let's establish that.

We were well schooled
in yes sir's, and no ma'am's,
in following rules, aware of authority,
knew our place, yet were adaptable.

In our dress and speech we wore
a cultural camouflage to fit into
new situations, changes in geography,
spoke with new accents or slang,
learned the lay of the land quickly
tried never to look out of place or lost.

We thought of ourselves as worldly
even living inside fences topped
with concertina wire, where guards
stood at gates, and when retreat sounded
we stood at attention hands over our hearts.

The DoD said we were resilient: easily made

new friends, were at ease in new situations,
wore our brat label with pride, all of that's true,
except there is so much they didn't say,

so much they didn't know, and so much we
didn't know ourselves. We did not know
how to voice our fears, we wore an armor
of denial we weren't aware we'd layered on.

There was sadness in not having hometowns,
not being able to have lifelong friendships,
attending too many schools, and always saying
goodbye, but we buried that deep inside, and
marched on with our heads up, shoulders back.

DEADHEADING ROSES

Love thou the rose, yet leave it on its stem
—Edward G. Bulwer-Lytton

Deadheading roses my bucket fills with fragrant
petals, falling from fingertips, their cascade
fosters recollection of little girls in a bridal party,
myself one of them, carrying beribboned baskets,
scattering rose petals down the center aisle in an
Air Force base chapel at Nellis.

The bride didn't know the little girls—we were
recruits—cherubic decorations to scatter rose petals,
soft, moist rose petals cool to the touch, and fragrant,
so fragrant, creating a rose petal path for the bride and
groom's first steps in married life.

Deadheading roses I am six years old again, a flower girl,
one among many traipsing down an aisle, but saddened
by desecration of roses wondering where in a tumbleweed
dry desert world so many roses were found to strip from
bud and stem filling baskets to the brim.

White Fence

The white fence around the pasture
looked Kentucky bluegrass good
when the house was purchased—
but it was built all wrong by a man
who knew nothing about fences
or the problem of keeping them
upright, wire brushed and painted

The fence did not so much
hold animals in—as hold them out,
as if animals would enter
the field the fence encircled

My mother did her best
to keep that fence white
and pristine—it was a drinker—
gallons of white paint it guzzled
and maybe for a time
painting it was therapeutic
allowed her to settle and sort things
in her mind but . . .

Finally one year
she gave it up, perhaps like
Tom Sawyer all gladness had left her
and a deep melancholy settled down
upon her spirit, she let the fence go
to yellow-gold lichened splotches,
silvering wood, and rotting posts
the next owner hauled away

TRACES OF CHRISTIE

Had it been a crime scene I scrubbed it clean—
1930 Sioux, Luke Air Force Base, Arizona.
I lived there from twelve to almost seventeen—
I changed from pixie cut hair to bouffant Bardot,

my stick figure gained height and a few curves.
I scrubbed bathroom floor tiles one-inch square
with a toothbrush and Clorox to whiten grout.

I scrubbed with a vengeance, an Air Force brat
daring white-gloved inspectors to find one settled
dust mote, one stain, one fingerprint, any minute
trace of our habitation there.

It was my last compliance to rules and regulations
within chain link fences topped by concertina wire
containing a military reservation and culture I knew.

I scrubbed with intensity and focus, didn't allow myself
to think about moving away, what it would mean for me
except another round of goodbyes, and those I couldn't
muster; something inside of me froze in that place of hot
summer days and sensuously warm summer nights.
I scrubbed away memories of my first French kiss,

my joy in riding horses, security of a steady boyfriend,
and an insouciant persona developed to get by when I
put on teenage armor and boxed up my sensitive side.

I scrubbed away a teenager who threw large parties,
had a head full of phone numbers for a gang of friends,
and loved going to Stage 7 in Phoenix to dance for hours.

I became a busy automaton, and months later I missed the girl
replaced by a zombie me going through the motions of life
when my dad retired from the USAF and moved his family north.
No one noticed Christie had been left behind, and no one rose up
to take her place, fill her shoes, and I wonder was she really me,
or only who I thought I should be, and does it even matter now?

OUR MOTHERS' LAUNDRY

—1950s Nevada

Our mothers hung laundry out with care, pegs in mouth
they had their techniques: knew which pieces shared a clothes pin,
which were heavier and had to hang alone. They used discretion—
undergarments hidden from view. They had high hopes dust storms
wouldn't kick up, good weather would hold, but there were kids,
watchful, willful, unpredictable and so very fast.

We were sun-darkened dusty desert brats skimpily dressed,
the temptation of wet laundry hung out to dry was too great for us
to pass by, so we ran at the laundry like little bulls—heads down
boring into shirts, shorts, towels, and the unmentionables—
ran though sheets brushing our bodies with refreshing moistness,
a sweeping caress, ran as swiftly as we could masquerading as wind.

SILVER DOLLAR SPOILS

Friday night's silver dollar spoils
stood in columns two or three abreast
catching Nevada's sunbeams
on my parents' chest of drawers.

My fingers nudged tall towers of coins
cool to touch often—maybe willingly—
toppling them to the sound of silver spilling,
splashing, skidding across polished wood.

On tiptoe I tried to recreate the columns,
the silver disks large in my small hands.
Stacking the coins without bulges, pausing
now and then to see Liberty's face, fingering
the coins ridged edges or oily smoothness.

I already knew about losers, lost paychecks
and old Lady Luck—fascination and fear
festered deep inside along with feelings
later discerned as loathing for gambling
and the place called The Las Vegas Strip,
curiously, there was my own compulsion
on Saturday mornings to always check
the winnings—or lack thereof.

For Dana Irish

In our desert days when we were young,
you rode Apache, a long-legged paint,
and I rode Cupid, stocky but sure,
a pretty little sorrel.

What a feeling to go from a bouncing
trot, to waves of a lope, when we made
the dust fly and went home gritty—
scent of horse upon us.

We rode early, just after dawn, sometimes
bareback, when we stole the horses
out of their pens at the OK Corral, it probably
wasn't okay to do that, but we brushed
those horses, cleaned them up good
and felt we'd paid our way.

Now that desert is all houses and streets.
I'm glad we had those rides, with miles
of open space, two daughters of fighter pilots
for our flights of imagination.

We were desperadoes. You—an Indian
Princess abducted from your tribe—me,

your freckled-faced companion and in those
desert days we knew freedom. We lived to ride
with abandon, hair flying back, our hands lightly
holding the reins.

SORTING CARROTS IN ARIZONA

We could have lolled about at a base swimming pool,
worked on our tans, sipped Coca Cola's, but instead
we went looking for real jobs the summer of '65.
The babysitting blues finally had us: late nights,
low pay, liquored up husbands driving us home.

Dawn went straight to Grand Avenue, said her sister
had a job at a plant along there that paid real well.
Dawn wanted to save to buy a car, me, I was along
for the ride, a comfortable one with leather seat luxury,
in six weeks I'd move to Washington State anyway,
but we were hired by the Navajo Packing Company
on Grand Avenue, and started work the next morning.

The packing shed was filled with Mexican women
young and old, bellies to conveyor belts, some sorting
carrots, others slipping bunches into plastic bags.
Young men loaded freight cars, otherwise lay about
on gunny sacks in the shadows, or bummed cigarettes
whenever we had breaks mostly to use the toilet.

Dawn lasted only a few days, but I stayed on, and only
in hindsight realized I was really hiding out. Because standing

at a conveyor belt sorting carrots—many shaped like gnarled
hands or something worse—and pitching them into a gunny sack
in front of me, letting perfect straight-arrow carrots go on by
to baggers—kept me from sorting out my feelings of my dad
retiring from the Air Force, and our leaving Arizona my home
of five years, because I was about to leave everything I knew.

Every once in a while I turned to smile and nod at the Mexican
woman beside me, so short she stood on a box. Every once
in a while we laughed at items on the belt, items lost in the fields,
and at those really strange carrots, honestly, who even knew they
grew that way, the imperfect ones must all be pureed for baby
food or juice, they sure didn't sell them in supermarkets like that.

We didn't stop working until the trucks quit rolling in, they
came beds heaped high with carrots; we'd watch the sky darken
through the big bay doors, and at some achingly tired point
when it felt like the trucks would never stop a Mexican woman
would begin to sing, and one by one all the rest would join in,
and their music filled the packing shed to the rafters and pierced
my heart.

DYSART REUNION 1966

In imagination

I return

to that rural school

Dysart,

surrounded by cotton fields

in Maricopa County

Solidly built of brick

it would remain

while I would not

stay in one place

ever so long

In imagination I say hello to:

Lupe Arriola

Roseanne Thompson

Flora Perez

Boni Reser

and Margie Villareal,

their names

a song of youth

In imagination,
I wonder
what became of them
and others

We were mostly transients,
farm workers' children or military brats

Many would be grandparents
now, even great grandparents,
or some may have their names
inscribed on that long
black wall in Washington D.C.,
or lesser stones

Others may be like me,
moved away, scattered like sand
after a wind storm, and how could we
ever celebrate reunion
except in imagination?

Moving Days (Air Force)

and there it was, gaping mouth
of a moving van ready to swallow
all household goods, even toys,
a tongue-like ramp into the dark maw,
moving men walking up it wheeling
barrels of dishes, furniture, boxes,
shadeless lamps—as the van filled—
the house emptied—became a place
for echoes, of small lost items found
behind appliances or furnishings and
dust bunnies set free to drift about
adding to the sense of abandonment

we kids on the block carried on with
games of tag, of hopscotch, or jacks,
surreptitiously eying the progress
of husky men handling belongings,
ours, or those of our friends

if the moving van was there for us
we pretended it was not, pretended
nothing had changed or would change,
for just as long as we could keep up
this facade and ignore the inevitable

which would mean goodbyes and
acceptance we were moving away

once everything was transferred
from house to van, after it pulled away
there was still cleaning to do,
then a motel or transient barracks
to stay in, then driving away forever
because we were being transferred—
which meant this place we'd come to
know was now part of our past
and knowing we had no choice in this
we did not glance over our shoulders
for one last look

KOREAN WAR MEMORIES

In 1952 Korea was for me an unimaginable
somewhere, a faraway place my dad flew
Checkertailed F-86es in hot pursuit of MiGs.

He'd shot down two, my brother Simon showed
how holding balsa wood airplanes for a reporter
who'd come to our house on Byron Street.
Our photo appeared in the Bellingham Herald
with an article about the hometown hero,
today a yellowed clipping redolent with decay.

In the photograph we're seated on the satin striped
sofa, I'm hugging a Chinese doll close to my chest,
our mother cradles the new baby, Shaun, to hers,
he had yet to meet our father, my daddy.

This memory replays of my confusion at age four:
sitting alone on that sofa legs and feet sticking out,
rocking back and forth puzzled by that place called
Korea, a place so far away my daddy couldn't come
home at night to swing me high upon his shoulders.

I'd seen the Pacific Ocean, knew he was beyond it,

but all I envisioned was steel grey sea, and heavy sky

sealed by an impenetrable line of horizon.

THE HOMECOMING

When my dad came through the door—home
from cross-countries or extended tours of duty
without us—he filled the house, his voice louder
than my mother's, his movements demonstrative,
less predictable. About him a whiff of beer, whisky,
sweat, or all three combined. He would take stage,
as they say in theatre, and be the center of attention.

His B-4 bag would thump to the floor—that magical
military suitcase so ahead of its time in design—
it was zippered, soft-sided, both garment bag and
multi-pocketed wonder it kept all the military man's
regalia in decent press, and well-organized. He could
easily find his orders, underwear or shaving kit, and
he would secret gifts in it to extract like a magician.

Gifts from Japan came in finely crafted lidded boxes
made of white-blonde wood smooth to touch with
a tantalizing scent that sent me someplace distant and
exotic, or perhaps it came from the packing materials
of curled wood shavings, nestled in them were gifts;
I remember a red lacquered wooden doll for me.

Once there was a half-carved rosewood Buddha,

just his bald head, round belly and a jagged wing
of wood. The carver was ready to toss him away
but gave him to my dad instead. That Buddha traveled
with us for years, even across the Atlantic and back.

When my father came home he would be almost
a stranger, we knew he belonged but a sea change
would occur, my mother demoted in rank shed
her command and like us fell to and took his orders.

We all had adjustments to make and sometimes
did so begrudgingly once the excitement of him
was over and we longed for our laid-back routines
without him, until the change became the ordinary
drill when my dad came home every day.

My Mother's Wish

She said someday her ship would come in—
in the chaos of mornings getting three children
off to school—first, nagged out of bed:
there was breakfast to prepare, lunch money
to dispense, permission slips to be signed—
mentioned at the last minute and misplaced
somewhere in the bottom of someone's bag.
Always, always, the chaos of "hurry, hurry, hurry,"
to catch a school bus. God forbid she would need
to drive us to our separate schools—
that was not how she wanted her day to go.

She said someday her ship would come in and
it almost sounded like a threat. Would she stand
on a deck waving goodbye as a gangway dropped?
Would there be streamers with us, her children,
standing holding onto ends of it tearfully watching
our mother sailing away waving her handkerchief
and laughing hysterically? It gave us reason to pause
now and then.

She said someday her ship would come in when her husband
moved the family to his hometown, Bellingham, leaving her
in a new place without friends, with few neighbors and all

responsibilities when he left to take a job overseas.
There faced with frustrations, anxieties, a house on five acres,
and three teenagers to look after on her own she muttered,
"Someday, someday, my ship will come in."
Then one day it did, a 45-foot commercial fishing vessel
the Laverne II, a troller, where she became First Mate
on the Pacific Ocean, cleaning and icing fish,
doing laundry, running the boat, cooking, still cooking
all the meals, and washing up, but no kids by then,
we were all grown and pretty much on our own.

They say, be careful what you wish for—I am.
I remember sending my mother letters care of
F/V Laverne II in ports of Southeast Alaska,
and on the coast of Washington, and even
more clearly I remember her letters to me.

PART 2

TRAVELING SHOES

THE ROYAL HUDSON

At the window of Fairhaven Library
looking towards Bellingham Bay I saw her
round Post Point, a plume of white smoke
making a 45 degree bend above her stack,
jet black engine gleaming in sunlight.

Momentarily, the sighting felt normal
as if witnessed on a daily basis
despite my being mesmerized by it,
then, I realized—I lived in another era—
in another time.

Hadn't I read somewhere the steam train
Royal Hudson made a special trip to Seattle
and now was returning home to Canada?

Yet I've often wondered about
the moment I saw her
how she felt so familiar,
so much a part of my life—
had she been one day,
one life before?

TUNNEL VISION

You don't think of Monet's garden divided,
oh, most certainly the flower beds
in long rectangles, every inch planted,
separated by rose-quartz gravel walks,
espaliered apples form a low twining fence
near *La Maison* in the *Clos Normand*, but voilà
down a stairway, through a tunnel you will go
in search of the famed water lilies,
the wisteria-draped Japanese high arched bridge.

In Monet's day, he simply walked across railway
tracks to his *basin aux nympheas*. Somehow, I wonder,
had it been there, would he have painted the tunnel
interior of water lilies closed at night,
or did Monet, with his failing vision, need light to open
his eyes to paint reflections, and his beloved lilies, canvas
after canvas after canvas? Would the tunnel have been
like total blindness or death, and much too far
from the light?

NORMANDY DAY 1

So, there we were 12 tourists sitting in the garden of La Poterie.

Awaiting the keys to that well-shuttered stone farmhouse

Which didn't look as splendid as advertised, concerns about it surfaced:

Someone discovered the barbecue to the side of the house rusted and filled with water,

was it an omen of what was inside?

Someone opened a bottle of wine passing it around.

Someone else brought out paper cups for sanitation or decorum.

Someone wondered aloud, would the house have heat, electricity and

functioning bathrooms?

Old telephone poles at the back of the house were wireless, we spotted the pole

carrying wires we hoped were live.

Still, there were two fallen down structures beside the house, more mysteries.

We were near the village of St. Evroult, but were most truly in the country.

To say we sat in a garden stretches the truth quite a bit.

Someone had gardened there once. Later in the season roses would bloom by the door;

quince blossoms had come and gone.

Just as we would come and go, just as the British owners apparently had done.

We were in *La Selle* (the saddle), the lay of the land holding the mid-nineteenth century house built by the Hubert family who made *camembert*, living first in the now fallen down *columbage longere* overgrown by trees, with vines penetrating the walls widening cracks. Time, weather and nature working to bring the structure down. It sheltered the owners as they worked themselves into prosperity, in 1850 building the mansion with two stories, in 1930 adding the third.

When the keys arrived we were all too eager to investigate, rushed through the doorway to see the place where we would live. Much relieved to find functioning bathrooms, three in all, seven bedrooms quickly claimed, bags toted in, shutters carefully opened.

We had traveled far to get here, twelve of us, mostly strangers, two couples, a few friends, but most of us had never met and now would be together sharing mealtimes, bathrooms, automobiles, and new adventures. Some early risers, some late, but no matter, the birds in Normandy sing all day from the trees and hedgerows, even the cuckoo.

Our first night preparations for a meal began only to have the gas go out, and so we made do with bread and Nutella, cheese, fruit and drink, happy we had eaten *croque monsieurs* late in the day in *L'Aigle*, ready to unpack our bags, test the beds and settle in.

MERCREDI 13 MAI 2009

Giverny, Monet's garden after 1700 heures

There is a rush hour in the town of Giverny, incessant noise
of traffic makes its way into Monet's garden until eventually,
thankfully, it subsides, sounds of the garden again audible: honey
bees so heavy-bodied it's a wonder they fly, they bobble from flower
to flower, a smörgåsbord of color and scent, they hum in bass
chorus with higher pitched chirping birds that flock to this garden
to feed on seeds, where there is water to sip and dip in.

Close to Monet's house, espaliered apple trees blossom, how
easy it will be to pick the fruit from the well-cultivated low cordon
of intertwining limbs. Tulips show wear of wind and rain, stained
petals curl, they are fading beauties.

Alliums with straight, tall stems support large globular heads
attracting butterflies. Peonies with tightly knotted heads offer a
burlesque peek at colors they will unfurl. Whereas giant peonies,
gloriously Rubinesque, display ball gowns of ruffled petals. Would
Monet mind that description, I wonder?

I sit in his garden on a bright green bench wondering where
he would have been on an evening such as this. I imagine him
on pebbled walkways, would he hear voices in the kitchen, the
clattering of pots and pans and stop by to investigate? Or would he
head to his *Jardin D'eau* for a last look at his beloved water lilies in

slanted light? I stroll the paths myself making my own scrunching sounds until I settle again.

Garden carts laden with potted plants await the gardeners like palette dabs of color. Spent flowers come out, new plants are set in and it's always show time here. The work Monet began, and gave decades to, goes on. With the sweat of his brow, he and his family created a landscape he would later paint, and fortunately those that loved his work reconstructed his garden so we can be a part of his landscape, his *Clos Normand* his *Jardin D'eau.*

LA PARISIENNE,

THEN AND NOW

The women of Paris hold their heads high

Their fashion is timeless

They have the eye,

Their carriage is that of a princess or queen,

Through much walking and diet

They are very lean.

The women of Paris buy not for one season,

They select clothing of quality

Which is a very good reason

For them to buy whatever suits them best,

Flattering their bodies being part of their quest.

The women of Paris always dress well,

No sweat pants for them—

Not for Renoir's Henriette H., or any *La Belle*!

THE SEINE

In the bustling, busy city of Paris
Of cars, pedestrians, bicyclists,
Buses and so many gawking tourists,
The walkways along the river Seine
Below street level at waters edge
Whether Rive Droite or Rive Gauche
Provide a pleasant escape from crowds.

Strolling beside the slow moving Seine
On a wide cobblestone walkway
Smoothed by the steps of millions
There are discoveries:
Iron gated passageways to buildings,
Great iron rings to tie up barges,
These stir up thoughts linked
To the history of the quays.

Sit on the benches and observe
The river traffic, the various barges,
Some taking visitors short distances,
Others hauling cargo afar to distant
Ports of call. Drift in sensations
Not found on city streets or alleys,
In the bustling, busy city of Paris.

NORA

She rides a bicycle in her dreams
on the country lanes of County Meath
pedaling her way to dances: Gossip
with the girls, flirtations with boys
smelling of soap, hair slicked back,
shyly standing across the dance floor,
jostling one another as young men
will do.

She rides a bicycle in her dreams,
the season is always springtime,
the hills are never steep,
she speeds along, until a cock's crow
creates a schism splitting the dream
world into memory, she awakens
with a curious longing, at home,
but far from home.

She listens to the hum of the interstate,
contemplates her morning cup of tea,
once more the rooster sounds his rousing
call turning the world into countryside,
but nothing like the country lanes
of County Meath.

MY BEIJING FRIEND

She crossed my mind this morning,
the woman in Beijing standing
on the balcony of a high rise,
not one that appeared to be
an ice cube tray on its side with small
slots for occupants, it was far better,
more upscale, and I was standing
in a parking lot with tour buses,
at one of many factory outlet places
they hauled us to so we would spend
money, but I did not want to shop,
instead what I came away with was
this memory of looking up and up
and seeing the woman on the balcony,
I waved to her and she waved back,
and for a moment our connection felt
as if we had clasped hands and she
had graciously invited me in for tea.

TRAVELING WITH MITFORD'S EDNA ST. VINCENT MILLAY

Edna traveled with me from Seattle to Miami.

Up the coast we went to Delray Beach

To visit my relatives, not hers.

She yawned at this, how preferable

Her Cora would have been.

She rustled her pages by the familiar

Ocean breeze of the Atlantic. That stirred

Memories: the cottage at Camden, Maine.

The disaster at Sanibel, her manuscript

Lost when the Palms Hotel burnt down.

Displaying she was restless, she fluttered,

Always there was the pensive, level stare,

Chin cupped in her hand she took in

The surroundings, the gated houses

Their elegance would suit her well,

She would be at home in the moneyed estates,

Beyond the well-landscaped lawns and palm trees

She could be pampered on night stands,

Rest, or flirt with the man or woman of the house,

Or both, she would let him or her hold her against

silken sheets, against willing thighs and immediacy.

She would give sidelong glances to their mates,
As their fingers spread her pages, she would
Shiver in delight, and so would they, so would they.
They would plunge into her poetry, her lovely light
Burning. Yes, yes, her words were all for them.

At least for that moment, for one or the other,
As long as they held her, as long as she desired
Being held. When I packed her in my bag, she was
Willing to travel in darkness, oh, she knew about
Darkness, but once in Key West she escaped,
Maybe tired of my abstemious ways she was going
To burn that candle, she was going to burn it
Long, and she was going to burn it bright.

PART 3

OBSERVATIONS

Cordial with Ms. Crow

Most mornings I feed a crow
small tidbits, minute scraps,
my handouts won't sustain her,
she meets her own dietary needs:
forages on Little Squalicum beach,
eats worms, picks through garbage cans,
seasonally finds fallen fruit, insects,
robs nests of eggs and hatchlings,
this last habit of hers annoys me.

Crow moistens some of her food stuff
in a bird bath we provide, the water
turns into a bouillabaisse of sorts
but not one you or I would care to eat,
odd squiggly bits, broken pieces of shell,
all in a swill of murky rust-red water.
I scrub and refill the bird bath frequently.

Then crow breaks shellfish
on our driveway, airdrops these,
it can be dangerous out there.

Crow knows when I awaken,
trains her black pearl of an eye on me

just outside my kitchen window as
she sidles back and forth along a wire
curling and uncurling thready toes
while I drink my morning coffee,
frequently cocks her head as if
questioning when I'll come outside.

When I walk out to get our newspaper
she flies alongside me, wings pulsing
a steady beat in the stillness of morning,
and I feel an invisible string between us.

JAKE

—1997-2011

My cat returns in dreamland making his usual pause
inside the doorway before softly jumping onto the bed,
there's a weighted feel of him as he makes his way to nest
on the pillow I never use beneath the goose-neck lamp.

At night, while I read, he curled there, it was his sunshine,
he slept beneath the warmth of it contentedly,
sometimes purring—the noise as melodious
as stream water riffling over rocks.

My cat returns in dreamland, he is my ghost cat,
my furred hot water bottle, my soothing songster,
his brazen strides across the terrain of my body
were part of our nightly routine.

No longer can I reach out to trace his body,
my fingers sliding between his ears down his neck
feeling the curvature of his satiny, striped back,
he is now well beyond my grasp.

HOWL

—to Remember Allen Ginsberg and My Magnificent Dog Rudy

On moonlit nights, with a silvery path

Across Bellingham Bay, I am led to silliness

I can't explain except I'm a Cancer, the Moon

Has influence on me. So, I try to teach

My Standard Poodle Rudy

How to howl at the distant bright white orb.

I kneel beside him, throw my head back,

Pucker my lips out big, and round and work

The howl from deep inside: resonant, loud, and long,

Ahrooooooo, Ahrooooooo, I demonstrate.

His eyes sparkle with moonlight and merriment,

An intelligent dog he knows

Something is expected of him, so

He wags, and wags and wags his

Short curly bottle-brush of a tail,

Grins an open-mouthed toothy grin

With lolling tongue, but no attempt

To form the sounds of his canine forebears.

Still, he watches me patiently and listens

To my melodic howls.

CONSTRUCTION DOGS

Construction dogs adjust to new boundaries—
the job site is where their truck is,
where their human is, a daytime home
where the smell of sawdust is familiar
and sawed-off ends of two-by-fours
serve as toys to fetch or gnaw upon.

Construction dogs don't mind noise—
they're used to nail guns and electric saws,
boom boxes blaring, talk and laughter—
they don't usually mind other dogs on site,
this is not their territory to defend,
they sniff one another and make peace.

Construction dogs like going to work—
traveling with their heads out of windows,
or standing in the bed of a truck
shifting their weight as needed,
sniffing familiar scents on some roads
processing new information on others.

Construction dogs have a swagger—
they'd wear tool belts if they could—

they love houses that are framed up

still open to the sky and air,

being on the job site, that's their work,

and being ready to go, anytime, anywhere.

Watching the Storm

With wind gusting to 45 knots, waves on Bellingham Bay
roil grey-green and formidable, they slap
over the breakwater, in a white foaming froth.
Spindrift shoots southeast out of Hale's Pass dousing
the Lummi shoreline, obscuring Eliza in a veiled mist.
This is a day to be inside, onshore and cozy,
sipping coffee, keeping a weather eye out of curiosity,
not out of necessity, feeling solid footing
instead of riding the swells. A stout green and white
Foss tugboat with a bone in her teeth
hastens towards Fairhaven on a mission
to retrieve a barge broken free of its moorings.
Watching the tug's determined course in such a
tempest, I think of the crew and speculate whether
they sip coffee, and talk of sports, or other storms,
and if for them this is all in a day's work?

December Snow

We've had this time of snow
but especially the light—
the silver crystalline glisten of it
illuminating our days,
which had been up until then
endlessly grey, wet, and sullen.

The transformation welcomed,
even after nightfall when the old orchard
trees: filbert, pear, and apples
cast sinuous, but strong shadows
across the milk-blue snow.

Where usually there is darkness—
every inch of the yard was visible.

Awakened and out of my bed
in the middle of the night,
I paused at the window struck
by the stillness and lambent light outside—
stood in appreciation until chilled,
fully satiated by snow-bright surroundings.

WITNESS TO WINTER SAILINGS

On rare occasions south-westerlies kick up—
a scene of sailboats safely at anchor in Fairhaven
changes when three or four drag anchor, break away
and without any hand on tiller or wheel they
sail across Bellingham Bay in a messy business
of pitching and rolling in whitecaps, sail covers
unwrapping, sails unfurling and lines whipping.

Good luck for owners occurs if an anchor drags
in shallows, finds holding ground, digs in,
catches and stops a boat from catastrophe
yet to come—those boats reaching the far shore
go aground at Little Squalicum and are thrashed
against riprap sharp as a sea serpent's teeth.

The worst ravages are scavengers watching
the boats progress, they descend upon them
taking whatever they can plunder before high winds
and waves pummel and pummel hulls, breaking
them into smaller and smaller pieces, driving
stainless steel stanchions deep into rip rap crevices
nothing left except someone's memories.

PORT OF BELLINGHAM

Where once a working waterfront thrummed
and the noise of it never met complaint—
daily the Shipping News tantalized locals with
names of far and distant ports, as did exotic names
painted on ship's hulls.

Seasonally, the large fishing fleet: purse seines, trollers,
draggers, gillnetters and crabbers, were annually blessed,
sent off to fish herring, halibut, salmon, sole, and crab—
with smaller gillnetters staying close to home,
lighting up Bellingham Bay at night like a floating village.

The maritime traffic bustling in and out of the bay
was normal, as were stout harbor tugs towing freighters
or rafts of logs for the mills. That traffic has almost ceased;
instead, in its place, we have acres of blindingly white-hulled
yachts and sailboats, most never leaving their slips.

Winter days the bay is a slate of grey-blue water
plied only by seagulls, Canada geese, or possibly
a kayaker practicing skills.

NOSTALGIA

Sometimes I miss *Chérie*, our sailboat.
I miss the night sky in quiet coves
in Canadian waters where stars
were a net above us, and yet there were
satellites as well and their trajectory
could be followed with amazement
at what was far beyond while a stir
of bioluminescence illuminated the sea
and astonishment at what was right there.
I miss the simplicity of mere necessities:
my bunk, my cache of books and chocolates,
small galley and supply of food and drink,
the snug feeling of existing in our own world
within that cradle of boat, Amphitrite rocking
us to sleep. Yes, sometimes I miss *Chérie*.

Saturday Morning in Spokane

Saturday morning in Spokane walking to Auntie's Bookstore,
I pass by a cafè and the scent of bacon and eggs emanates from it
strong, and you can almost taste it and hear the waitress ask
"Would you like anything else hon', maybe a warm up on your coffee?"

That's the scent of America, the smell of bacon and eggs,
that's the sound of America, hon', and I look to the top of a building
spy an American flag whipping in the breeze, and everywhere,
almost everywhere you look in this city is a tower or a post
and on it is a great big clock with the correct time.

On the corners early, street people gather and shuffle their feet,
and I mean no disrespect to them, I just wonder, how do they feel,
when they pass by that place that smells so strongly of bacon and eggs,
and how many times in a day or in a week does anyone call them hon'?

Saturday morning in Spokane, Washington my stomach filled,
I've eaten Snoqualmie Falls oatmeal, drunk several cups of coffee,
and the waitress did call me hon' and I didn't mind that,
it's like the British calling you luv, it feels kindly.

Saturday morning in Spokane, Washington walking to Auntie's Bookstore,
I feel fortunate I can read, fortunate I can buy books,

fortunate I can buy a cup of coffee, sleep in a warm bed,

look to our flag and still feel proud of my country because I know

there are people like the waitress that give service with a smile,

there are people who show up for work each day

who care about doing a good job, and they pay their taxes,

and maybe we should just stop shouldering this entire burden—

tell the corporate giants it's time for them to do some good

with all the money they don't pay in taxes hon'.

If they did, maybe those fellows on street corners might have a bed,

might eat a good breakfast, might have a job, or get the help they need.

That's what I thought as I walked to Auntie's in Spokane, Washington,

the smell of bacon and eggs lingering in the air.

BIBLIOPHILE

There are times I am lost without a book,
or finish one and feel bereft, deserted
by all the characters whose acquaintance
I have made, whose homes I have visited,
whose thoughts and emotions coursed
through my body, triggering synapses,
sometimes breathless moments of tension.

Even though I have a Kindle and like it,
I prefer the printed page, the heft of a
printed volume. I carry books with me
if I might stop for coffee, or for security
just in case I must wait somewhere,
like recently at a John Deere dealership,
while my partner talked shop I sat content
with a book in my lap harvesting words.

EASTERN WASHINGTON,

THE PALOUSE

Demeter used her breath to blow
loess in, covering Columbia River Basalt
200 feet deep, she shaped it into a
female curvaceousness, sensuous
and giving, creating this fertile land where
bunchgrass once grew—now wheatlands
as far as the eye can see pattern the hills.

The French called this land *La Pelouse*,
it was all grasslands in the 1800s,
which told some settlers this was land
they could use for dryland crops.

But on the road to Steptoe Butte
card teasel lines the roadway
telling a story of other early settlers,
sheepherders, they brought the plant
from the old country for carding wool—
here in the Inland Empire where sheep
once grazed.

Gigantic machinery dominate the hills
plowing, seeding, cutting.
Seasonally the panorama changes from
winter white, to mud browns,
tender greens, then acres of gold.

The rolling landscape offers glimpses
of farmsteads that appear to rise up
and then fall back into safe pockets
hidden from view, and somehow
I can never see enough to satisfy me—
a craving sets in to visit and revisit
this rolling land time and time again.

Life Cycles in the Methow

Born in winter, snow falling and sticking,
caping their mothers' backs, Black Angus
calves find their legs and some autonomy
frolicking with other calves, a band of youth
discovering their kind, and their world.

Close by an array of avian scavengers waits:
eagles, hawks, ravens and magpies roost
in cottonwoods by the creek overlooking
the birthing field, watching for afterbirth
to feast upon; they'll swoop down to ingest
placentas—a satisfying meal, nutrient rich—
it repays their diligence, fuels their bodies.

On Upper Beaver Creek long before signs
of spring—it's an almost monochromatic world—
with dashes of bright color: red, blue, yellow,
green and orange in idle farm machinery,
except a nearby rancher's New Holland
tractor bearing load after load of hay to his herd.

New life is born, life cycles sustained—
cows fertilize fields their feed will grow in,
satiate large birds about to settle into nests—

and we who witness this are not as separate
from it as it may seem sheltered in our houses
or automobiles—binoculars or spotting scopes
to our eyes.

FEAST

Ravens issue the invitation—a raucous one—
throaty voices calling over and over,
their circling flight provides the address,
some sit on fence posts awaiting their turn
but call out—oh, how delectable the feast—
in the deep snow a trail of blood,
is evidence of the coyote's last steps
near the base of a hill off Upper Beaver Creek.

Party crashers come: magpies, eagles—
the golden takes his place at the head of the table,
his body ratchets up and down, great beak
tearing flesh—the ravens and magpie nibble
at the periphery, but when the golden eagle
raises a taloned foot or shifts slightly
the smaller birds skitter out of range
of the great bird's talons or beak.

Nearby three bald eagles perch in trees,
a study in patience, they will take their turns—
the splayed body of the coyote diminishes
in size bite-by-bite as the birds feast,
and the remains provide sustenance
to less obvious nocturnal visitors, or insects

and will quietly decompose, but presently
the carcass and blood-splattered snow
is a busy, noisy place of birds big and small,
of hierarchies and appetites.

SNOWPLOW SIDEWALKS

The snowplow driver
leveled banks of snow
along our country road,
and it now appears
we have sidewalks,
a surprising sight
on this winding road
without a centerline
or fog lines—how curbed
and citified it looks—
changed into something
I wouldn't want it to be.

Pine Trees—Two Views

—With thanks to e.e. cummings

Above Beaver Creek
a snowy hillside against
whitened sky portrays
pine trees on a ridge line
like folded paper cutouts
snipped out of fog—
then spread wide—as if God
played with scissors.

A second look shifts
pine trees to the foreground,
snow and fog recede, the sweet
surprise of the unexpected vanishes—
a trick of light and perception
or "now the eyes of my eyes are opened."

In Envy of Ravens

In Utah's red rock canyons, wing beats of ravens resonate
a steady, but soft *whup, whup, whup,* as they fly overhead,
wings flashing as sun glints off their black bodies—black
as desert varnish or obsidian.

Ravens appear to rule the vastness of the Colorado Plateau
surveying it all effortlessly—flying to remote mesas
hoodoos, pinnacles, or buttes—perching on them to
scan the desert floor, or soaring and swooping above it all.

Whup, whup, whup, they fly by at eye level
traveling to places our eyes or feet will never take us.
Ravens know the niches and crevices, the secret places
and potholes that fill with water when it rains.

It's easy to envy ravens watching them circle
or engage in aerobatics, tumbling and playing on the wind.
Up to great heights they ascend, descending to the ground
to strut like nobles resplendent in their sleek black garments.

June in the Methow

This spring a heavy snow pack after two major fires turned large fir and pine trees into dark silhouettes with roots no better than metal Christmas tree stands. Runoff from swollen creeks and streams damaged properties, and closed part of Highway 20 in the Okanogan. My ears are filled by water music, an orchestration of Beaver Creek, kettledrum sounds of boulders rumble pushed along the creek bottom, a noise to give pause and warning. Up our road there's evidence of water's surging power: a road undercut, chewed on both sides where the creek overflowed, redirected itself into new or familiar channels, eroded soil deep down exposing cable buried well below the frost line. Asphalt crumbles like pie crust on the edges of Upper Beaver Creek Road beyond where Balky Hill Road T's into it.

The creek has spread wide, debris of fallen trees and limbs are slag heaps, piled high within the creek, diverting its coursing quest to meet the Twisp and Methow Rivers. Repairs are in order once runoff lessens. Until then I listen to full-throated music glad our house is high upon a bench, but that didn't save the lower field when Storer Creek decided to come our way carrying silt and grit across our fields and driveway.

Summer Storm 2013

For two nights lightning
lit up our world in strobe-light
flashes silver-grey, the world
inside and out appeared
like old photograph negatives.

Thunder made us huddle close,
the two of us and the dog, while
the noise rumbled much too close—
rain hitting the metal roof hard,
drumming, and drumming, and
through a slightly cracked window
an eerie whistle of wind, the same
made the Norway maple
called "crimson sentry" shake
violently—it was a sight to see.

Power failed, electronics beeped,
clocks stopped, and somewhere near
Rainy Pass in the North Cascades
rocks and mud slid over Highway 20
burying it twenty-five feet deep,
stranding some motorists.
After all the meteorological mayhem

the following day dawned clear,

our bird bath was full, a small washout

on the driveway required attention

and a need to windrow the cut alfalfa

was obvious, but for songbirds

all was again right in the world and

they filled the air with sweet sounds.

ABOVE ONION CREEK

On the La Sal Mountain Loop Road, up the hill
slim blackened trunks—leafless dark limbs—
sinuous and sculptural oak trees sadly

describe the devastation of fire.
The acrid smell of charred wood and ash
assault the senses instead of sage and juniper.

The fire could have been stopped,
except two women passing by were busy,
too intent on their own plans to report
a small brush fire they observed which soon
swept the area taking thousands of acres of
vegetation, spoiling habitat. Now burnt
trees stand testament to their selfishness.

What stands out in their minds?
Their pickup truck could not be saved.
The hurried two who might have helped
halt the conflagration were saved—at least—
that's what the locals say about

what happened above Onion Creek.

News from the Methow

Summer fires

—A selection from Postcard Poems, August, 2014

Postcard No. 1

Acres of the Methow
hillsides and drainages burnt—
blackened, some terra cotta
striped in red flame retardant
dropped to suppress
the Cougar Flat and
Carlton Complex fires'
sweep across ridgelines—
taking everything in its
path: pine and fir trees,
aspen and cottonwood,
sagebrush, bitterbrush,
wild animals, livestock,
bird nests and people's homes.

A weekender's house
on a hillside of Wolf Canyon
sports an orange-red roof,
windows well coated too,
and this blush of retardant

provides a rose-tinted look
at a changed landscape
that was a hellish place
when we evacuated at 3:00 am
July 17th and still the smoke
spires up and up in never ending
smoldering spot fires, back burns,
and new fires yet to be contained.

Postcard No. 4
After being evacuated
because of fire and thick smoke
flickering candlelight
provided light at a dining table
—without electricity it was essential—
but also a reminder of what we'd fled
even if flames were from tall white tapers.

I tried to think of them like candles
I purchased in France, in Catholic churches,
—vigil lights for silent prayers—
but found it easier not to think of them at all,
focused instead on eyes or lips
of those sitting across from me—
listened intently to their words, ignored

reflections of flames on windowpanes
or reflection on flames in memory's eye.

Finally, without power in the valley,
except when provided by generators,
I'd put a bucket of water by the toilet
to flush it if needed in the night,
and go to bed flashlight in hand.

Tucked into bed I felt safe, sheltered,
reading by a small pool of light
directed at pages, illuminating words
to take me away from flames on hillsides,
or speculation on what was saved,
what might be lost, or endangered,
the sight of the fire-scorched earth
and oppressive flames still dancing
at a distance that was still much too close.

Postcard No. 8
After the Cougar Flat fire
met the Carlton Complex fire,
after watching large plumes
far too many days
the Rising Eagle fire 8/1/14

was too much—
a blown tire on a trailer,
rim scraping pavement
sparks flying, igniting grasses,
a rapid spread of flame
taking 36 structures, 10 homes.

The next day wind whipped
dust and soot atop a hillside,
it looked so remote for a few seconds,
then our young trees went sideways,
visibility zero, elsewhere mature trees
fell or dropped limbs, power outages
resulted and many of us joked
"We're waiting for locusts."

Now there's the Bridge Creek Fire,
people's lives on standby waiting,
watching, praying, and yes,
making jokes, what else can we do?

Postcard No. 16
If we could export our smoke
as we do our apples and other
homemade, homegrown products

we'd have a bumper crop
to package up for smoked salmon,
pastrami, *Gruyère* cheese, beer, ribs
and other foods.

We'd have smoke for smokescreens,
for the military, movie industry,
politicians, crooks and anyone
in need of one, anyone at all.

Beware however, the acrid
smell of smoke, it stings
the eyes, just as seeing damage
done by fires brings tears
and sadness, and oh yes,
if we could export our sadness
we'd have much to send away.

But we are also rich in compassion
and helpfulness Methow made,
and let's hope our willingness
to reach out to others spreads
beyond our valley, beyond state lines,
just as our fire footprint spread
far too large this year.

Postcard No. 17

Where did the animals flee to

when the fires came,

what refuge could they take?

Where did Ginger Reddington's

two horses go? I want to imagine

them grazing somewhere safe.

There were Black Angus

on the open range trapped

up in Finley Canyon,

a few who made it out

with burnt hooves, but what

of the deer, coyote, wolf pack,

weasels, marmots,

and even rattlesnake

up in Pipestone Canyon

where the blaze came down

hastened by wind

devouring grasslands, sage,

pine trees and cottonwood.

We have yet to hear coyotes

at dusk calling from hillside

to hillside as they usually do.

We will be watchful and listening
for signs the Methow is rebounding
to what it was before the fire raged.

COOPER'S CONCERN

November 1, 2016

Our neighbor has a brush pile burning.
Tall flames gyrate as fire gobbles oxygen.
Our dog spies this anomaly in territory
he views as his, barks sharp warning
sounds and emits a series of low growls
before he shoots us looks of concern.

We tell him he's a good dog but ask him
to stop, letting him know we know, yet we
wonder does he remember the night we
nervously watched advancing flames
from the Cougar Flat fire which merged
with the Carlton Complex fire in 2014.

Does he remember tension-filled moments
of our evacuation, recall breathing smoke
that hung in the air for weeks afterwards
which the sun could barely burn through?

He walks to windows to the east and west,
surveys all views then lies down with an uneasy,
wary look in his eyes before he makes a few
muffled growls at this most unwelcome intrusion.

MORNING ON BEAVER CREEK

Twenty-two Canada geese in a ragtag line
fill a brief interlude with honking calls familiar
to the ear, yet the sound always conjures
a sense of longing.

My eyes follow their flight and hearkening
sounds until the sky clears of this beckoning
and I am left both enriched and diminished.

I think whenever I hear them a piece of my soul
ascends, falls into their slipstream and flies away.

WAITING

A pair of bald eagles were busy in February
in a dead cottonwood tree by Beaver Creek,
remaking an old nest that survived a fire.

I eyed it as I walked our puppy in the snow
on access to our loafing shed, he could have been
a meal for them to carry away. I kept him close.

At night I knew they were there, sometimes
heard their inexplicable chirpy staccato sounds
and appreciated their company in the dark.

They made preparations. We were watchful
of the nesting bird, her white head a marker
of her brooding presence and patience.

Her mate sat in another tree close by, and
we were as expectant as they might have
been, and longing to see little eaglet heads

peek above the lip of the twiggy nest, hopeful
we'd be lucky and see them fledge. But one day,
the white head visible for months disappeared,
her mate was gone as well, stillness enveloped

the nesting site and an emptiness that hollows
the soul filled us with speculation and sadness.

METHOW WEATHER REPORT

Today, ice thin as onion skin
formed between ribs on metal
rooftops, melted, as the day
warmed, slid slowly to eaves,
slipped off in small rectangles—

translucent postcards of capricious
weather fluttered down—
Jack delivered one to me
in the palm of his hand.

OREGON COAST

At Hug Point seagulls stand in a skim of water over sand;
it mirrors their antics. One snakes his head low, sips and then
head back, looks as if he will gargle fresh water trickling
across the beach to meet the sea. It spills down a waterfall over
a rock cliff draped in luminous algal green. A few gulls saunter
to the falls to drink, or bathe in the pool at its base.

One can envy seagulls at times like these, their abilities to fly,
float bobbing along in waves, and on this day or any to spend
all day in the embrace of this place without a need to check
the time, think about traffic on the interstate or deadlines.

Living on the east side of the state a visit to the ocean is rare,
so I slowly turn to look in all directions and like the seagull
slurping water try to fill myself with this place before a trip back
over the mountains to the shrub steppe and home.

PART 4

ADDRESS BOOK

Self-Acquaintance

If I must look back—and sometimes I must—
let me look into the corners of my life beneath
sofa and chairs, into all the places dust and
seldom-used objects collect.

If I must look back, let me see my life clearly,
without any drama about it, nor through myths
I've created. Instead, to face my life head on,
there's nothing so glaring it will blind me.

If I must look back, let me feel what I couldn't
feel when girded to defend choices or actions:
There I am in warrior pose. Beware.
Be wary of any posturing on my part.

If I must look back, let it be over my right shoulder using
my best eye, my feet planted, knees slightly bent.
Yes, I'm ready now, ready for anything, and nothing,
nothing will bring me down.

HER FINAL WISHES

She said to bury her with a teaspoon,
one that's become her perfect measure
for sugar in her many cups of tea.

My mother imparted this request as we sat
side-by-side in a small examining room waiting
for the surgeon who removed her right breast—
she chose that option to chase her cancer,
a prior lumpectomy unsuccessful.

We laughed over the teaspoon, just as we laughed
selecting her coffin, she wanted the "Sherman,"
the lowest priced coffin the funeral home offered.

We joked about it having tracks like a Sherman tank
and driving it across Woodlawn Cemetery into the plot
pre-purchased as her final resting place.

So far her wishes request a stark simplicity:

> Say little in an obituary; dress her in the grey robe;
> socks on her feet, a knit hat, rosary beads in her hands;
> no church service just graveside; absolutely no lilies—
> she detests them—in fact no flowers at all; family only
> except the Ziemba's, except now they're both deceased.

Only Atropos, who cuts the thread of life, knows
the full measure of her days; inside me a reservoir
of tears slowly fills as I add the teaspoon to my list.

LEAVING WASHINGTON

She left this world lightly,
any shred of vanity discarded,
content without her glasses or wig,
although she was delighted by the pink
Nike stretch pants I bought for her.

She did say once, *So it's come down to this.*
By which she meant her room with only
hospital bed and nightstand, a windowsill
covered with cards, vases of flowers, a few
photographs—no house to keep, no dinners
to prepare, death's door ajar.

She outlived her husband, outlived his need
for her care, and freed of that responsibility
for the first time in decades she could decide
her own course, so occasionally she looked
down and flexed her toes as if readying herself
to depart whenever she felt it was her time to go.

PARENTS

Maybe I was born to miss them,
hanging onto my mother's skirt
as she applied bright red lipstick
for an evening out when I was six
years old. Never really knowing
where my father was when he went
on cross countries—he was absent
enough weekdays, and weekends
taken up with his entertainments—
yet he had the heart of a family man,
in the sense that his family mattered
to him: his mother, aunts and uncles,
sisters, cousins, and maybe even us.

Maybe I was born to feel their absence early on
when left with babysitters at times, later
when they went away for travels and work,
a disconnect bridged by letters or phone calls.

Yet they lived long lives, longer than I would
ever have imagined, into their ninth decade.

On their demise there were some who said
in dismissive tones of voice that they were old,
like something worn out and easily discarded.

No one wants an expiration date on those
they love—even if it was their time to go—
missing them I am still a child holding onto
my mother's hem and my father's hand.

LOST & FOUND

Skin on my 94-year-old father's hands
flakes off in tiny quarter-moon crescents,
brushing this dander off black car seats
I face losing him bit-by-bit with his skin
so fragile.

On a recent outing we traveled
Chuckanut Drive to the Edison Tavern.
One section of familiar roadway
with jutting sandstone to one side
always sparked a recitation handed
down by his mother, my grandma Nelle.
As we rounded that 270-degree curve
I always heard a tongue twister:
Round and round the rickety rock . . .
but he was silent, and so was I.

One day late my father spoke up,
said he remembered something,
and began reciting:
Round and round the rickety rock
the raggedy rascal ran,
how many r's are in that
tell me if you can?

So there it was—momentarily—
his mother, my grandma Nelle
brought to life. I was a child again
and so was my dad, traveling wherever
we are headed on separate journeys filled
by routines, surprises, oftentimes losses,
but if there is grace—the blessing of
remembrance.

December Visit to Greenacres

—Johan Petrus (Pete) Anderson
1899 - 1960

On your grave, a molehill piled high,

the soft damp mound disconcerting,

as is grass overgrowing your marker.

Crisp, dry leaves skitter across the lawn

helter-skelter until a strong gust sweeps

them towards the gate.

I place the Christmas wreath down,

pegging it to the ground so the Nor'easter

won't blow it from here to who knows where.

Next time—next time—I'll trim things up here,

sweep away dirt filling letters of your name.

Next time—next time—I'll stay longer. Today,

it's bitterly cold, rain clouds head this way,

low and lumbering. Now, for a moment, just

before I rise I remember you on your knees

beside me on the oval braided rug, when you
would steal my nose, making me laugh until
my sides hurt and that memory warms me.

GRIEF

Grief, you arrive at the oddest moments:
on a sunny day while I am driving
down a two-lane country road—
a gambol of cumulus clouds move above
hills, gold arrowleaf and purple lupin
color them—and there you are
in all your mournful raiment
pointing your long finger at me.

At first you took me by surprise,
gobsmacking me when all was well,
but now I know to expect you
on occasion to single me out,
and I've heard from so many this sorrow
will continue for a lifetime, moments
of grief will come, but like an alchemist
I'll turn them into treasure.

ESTHER MARIA

(ANDERSON) KEEPERS

—July 17 1890-1957

For so many years I mourned the loss,
wondering why my great aunt Esther
had to die so young, lamenting
what might have been.

Funny, how hard it is to let go of those
you love, sad to remember her only
in a silent movie way, not being able
to recall her words, only her posture:
the way she stood with one hand
on her arched back surveying
the garden at her Whidbey Island home
perched high above the bay.

She always wore gloves when she drove
the cream-colored Plymouth, she possessed
that Swedish sense of tastefulness.

Traveling to her house we hailed
each passed landmark with cheers
building in crescendo, anxious to be

at Esther's again, anxious to turn
onto the Troxell Road and glimpse
the farm and feel homecoming.

Calculating Deaths

in the Family

When my last great aunt died it
registered
somewhere in my throat
a feeling of strangulation

then an aunt died, the probability
of death moved down to the next tier—
somewhere in my brain
an abacus bead slid over and clicked
against another, it would not move back,
a calculation was made—who remained—
who would be removed

the killer—cancer—answered the question
in its unkind way with certainty
taking another aunt slowly,
a death cloud hanging over her,
hanging over all who knew her,
with the whispered—*it's a matter of time*—
it is always a matter of time—

and as my generation ages,

there are still a few who came before us

but it is anyone's actuarial guess,

or calculation as to whom might go next,

who will outlive the other,

the abacus is there—

more beads will click into a new place

and not move back

sometimes this registers

in my chest with such tightness

it dawns on me there is so much more

I need to learn about acceptance

GRAVITY

—In memory of Evelyn Mason

Gravity, enemy of the elderly, awaits a fatal misstep,
pulls them down ungraciously, injures fragile bones:
hips, ribs, femurs, one or more, sets off a series
of conditions, conspires to take them to a final darkness.

And so it happens we find ourselves audience
at a "Celebration of Life," for an elderly, gifted friend,
we sit in stillness, listen to cello music, eulogy,
remembrances, view photographs, and admire flowers.

Sometimes the gravity is broken by memories
that amuse, and laughter is balm for distress—
creates a supportive bond as does saying
prayers in unison. Afterwards—

We join in fellowship, eat small sandwiches,
sip tea or coffee, see elderly friends and family
and wonder who among us might be next, falling
victim to a force that heretofore kept us earthbound.

CERTITUDE

Certitude: the word catches the eye

penetrates the brain, creates

a pause, a wondering

at what is certain

except uncertainty,

at least that's how I see it

For even my faith holds

great mysteries,

unknowns to contemplate

but never unravel

Yet the word

certitude

crops up

in my reading—

hits my eyes

smack on—causing me

to circle around

the word

again and again

I am a Vessel

Some people are made to weep,
cry silently, or sob without reserve,
even in public, they daub their eyes
then go about their business.

Others are reservoirs of tears—
genetics, upbringing—creates
a tendency in us to suppress.

I put my unspent tears down
to a Swedish-British reserve,
for reasons I do not know,
but I do know this:

People like me unable to cry
easily—well, we aren't less
lachrymose—we just won't let go,
but if we did our tears would fill
bathtubs, millions of pots and pans,
rain barrels, bottles stout or tall,
cups, steins, water or wine glasses,
bowls—even the dog's and the cat's—
vases, water troughs, wash tubs,
sinks—well I think you get the idea.

We are brimful, sloshing, containing,

retaining vessels, the wisest of you

would be wiser yet to wear waders

if you suspect a breach—our dam

giving way—for there will be a torrent

water will pool at our feet and rise

like the highest tide in a winter's storm.

UPDATE

Deleting the deceased
from my address book,
feels like another death,
a reminder a connection
has been lost as I erase
those written to or phoned.

Perhaps I need a book
of remembrance to list
them all, and a day to read
each name aloud, honoring
those I knew who've passed
on to an unknown address.

PART 5

TAKE AWAY

About this Stone

Sadness happens
to me so infrequently
that now, feeling it—
it is so unaccustomed
my chest cavity heavy as stone,
some high tide of emotions
tipping my balance,
and what is the cause
of this and my hunched
shoulders, and this
uncommon despair?

I don't know exactly,
I just don't know.

I have taken on a sorrow
like a damaged boat takes
on water and I list.
I need someone to
bail me out, or something to
buoy me up,
perhaps sleep would do it,
but I dare not crawl
into bed pulling the covers

over my head, I dare not
allow that, but then I ask myself,
why not? Why not wallow
in this sadness like a pig—

in a mucky sty, enjoy it to the fullest,
moan and groan, gnash my teeth,
do whatever it is depressed people do,
except become inebriated,
or jump off a bridge,
or cut photographs of myself
into thin strips. I could eat
all the ice cream I suppose,
but unfortunately I already feel
full, of that stone, of this sorrow,
of so much self-pity.

So I will sit with it, this uninvited guest,
and try to bump its shoulder with mine,
and jostle it, nudge it, tickle it under its chin,
and maybe we'll dance a polka around the house,
singing, *Ta ra, Ta ra.*

ACHING

I remember my heart feeling heavy
I was sluggish with the weight of it,
and that July the full moon was huge,
immense, brightly illuminating the bay.

Suicidal thoughts did come to mind—
at that time the Taylor Street dock
was just that, a refueling dock for tugboats,
not far from my house, easy to get to.

I could step off of it into the icy cold water—
Bellingham Bay doesn't warm in the sun
at that depth, but it didn't seem practical,
too easy to swim to shore if I changed my mind.

Deception Pass would do it, no turning back there.
Jump off that bridge into the swirling waters below
where the ashes of my grandfather were dispersed.
Yet I despaired at my own death, or my death wish.

I was much like a monk in my cell
performing self-mortification with my thoughts
of you with her—laughing, making love, deliriously happy.

Somehow I went on, although I did shed several pounds,
couldn't eat, smoked packs of cigarettes, bit my nails down.

It was as if I had ingested barbed wire.
I just hurt that much inside,
and that moonlight turned my skin blue.
It was a good color for me I thought.

DESIRE

At night in my bed
I long to swim
in almost tepid water
moving slowly at first
hands cupping resistance
as if clearing a pathway
for my head and torso,
legs and feet propel me
also.

Every night this occurs,
a desire to slip out of bed
miraculously discovering a pool
where I swim naked and alone,
swimming and swimming
until I tire and lift myself
out to lounge momentarily
by the lighted turquoise water
before toweling myself dry.

Then back to my bedroom I'd go
to sleep, in a body ready for sleep,
to sleep in a body ready for dreams.

To Sin By Silence

*—A poet once wrote: "To sin by silence, when we should protest makes
cowards of men." Of women too, I might add, of women too.*

If you visit the military cemeteries in France
Your breathing may become shallow seeing
Acres of land covered by crosses marking graves
For the fallen of World Wars I and II.

It's difficult for the mind to process so much loss,
Let alone the carnage in the mud: blood, guts, and
Cries of the dying for their mothers, deafening noise
Of shots, shelling, explosions, the sound of heavy
Machinery, the factory of war as it ground through
Long days and on into the night.

It's difficult to imagine all that, and also to think
It didn't end there, it never ends, untold numbers
Were never honored, were instead unceremoniously
Buried in pits like so much garbage, bones and skulls
To one day be recovered or not.

Some of us have seen too many war movies, too much
Coverage on the evening news of soldiers in camouflage
In jungles or deserts, or scenes of shell-pocked buildings,
The rubble of war zones, the wounded on stretchers.

Our reactions should register shock or outrage, or despair

Are dampened, an insular complacency, war and conflicts

Are all we've ever known, and usually happen far away.

I gasped at the sight of a dummy, an effigy in Normandy

Hung from the spire of Saint Mére Église, the 82nd Airborne

Stick lived to tell the tale, though deafened by church bells,

Still, I wanted to cut down his effigy, pull it to safety, and

Scream for all to hear, "Enough!"

DRILL

In the 1960s in Arizona at Dysart School
they loaded us into buses, all classes
first grade through high school,
small children sat on older children's laps,
rehearsed evacuations in case of nuclear war.

As if somehow they could load us all up
and drive to someplace safe from fallout,
we had these drills just as some had
fire drills, or earthquake drills, and always

it seemed they occurred on sweltering days.
We'd open windows to try and get some air,
and do our best to entertain the little ones,
who didn't understand the exercise at all
and maybe that was just as well.

And when the exercise was over, back we went
to our classrooms and tired history books filled
with wars, generals, policy makers and not many
peacemakers among them, and today jingoism is
the language of the day, and today the word fear
appears more often than peace, and today some
world leaders test missiles, as others test patience,

and you wonder if they ever learned the words

or outcomes of holocaust or Hiroshima, and looking

back on my own education I think perhaps a lot

was missed except these leaders never sat in buses and

wondered where'd they be at doomsday.

TOY SOLDIER

I found a plastic toy soldier,
knees slightly bent he stands
rifle held high overhead,
his stance suggests wading
through a river or a swamp.

Finding him by Highway 20
one thing was certain:
he was missing in action
—separated from his platoon—
I put him in my pocket.

I thought of soldiers who fought
in wars, some with fading memories
now still suffer nightmares of watching
friends fall and hearing their cries.

There are those who came home
from Vietnam to derision, those
who came home from other battles
to welcome home signs—yellow
beribboned trees—but part of them
remains trapped in wars far away.
I think how it never ends this business

of war—fabricating machinery for it,
reasons to engage in it, even factories
cranking out tiny plastic toy soldiers.

I rub the toy soldier between my thumb
and finger like a worry stone wondering
what it would take to manufacture peace.

ENEMIES

What did I know of enemies in the amniotic sea of my mother's womb? She was healthy, I thrived. What do I know six decades later?

During a torrential rainstorm when I was three, a neighbor parked his small car on higher ground so rising water wouldn't ruin it. Rainstorms equaled flooding requiring caution, I took note. My older brother slipped between two rowboats and almost drowned. Was water a foe?

When I was four living in Bellingham, my dad was in Korea flying F-86s; he shot down a MiG. A newspaper reporter came to photograph us; my brother Simon demonstrated with balsa wood planes what took place. Did it occur to me the MiG pilot was an enemy who died when his plane crashed, that my dad could have died? Did I begin biting my nails then? Parents died, I knew that.

My dad's dad drowned in Lake Samish. There was also disease. My mother lost her mother to cancer. I felt I needed to stay close to my parents, keep an eye on them. It was worrisome my dad was so far away. My parents are in their 90s today, still living in their own home. Fear can be an enemy, I know that now.

There were characters in books who were enemies: trolls under bridges, evil witches, wicked step mothers, a tiger that chased a little boy until he turned into butter. He did not frighten me, instead

I placed the book on the floor and ran in circles to see if I would turn into butter. I did not. These were fairy tales: my mother had real stories of enemies, of air raids requiring people to get out of bed, bundle up quickly and head to a shelter underground. It was World War II; she worked in a munitions factory in Peterborough, England. She told of a woman and child who didn't get up to head to the shelter and died in a bombing raid. Five years later, when I was nine, we lived in France, and Germany.

I saw the aftermath of World Wars I and II in acres of green grass with perfect straight lines of white crosses marking graves of those who died fighting wars. I saw leftover fortifications of war, a few bombed buildings, foxholes, and found German helmets in the Kile River we waded in. We were warned never to pick up anything that looked like a bomb, or munitions. The refuse of wars was dangerous to children's lives and limbs. War was a commonly used term. We lived in the Cold War era, and 1950s school children knew about air raid drills and backyard bomb shelters. Children like me who were raised on military installations were awakened by base alerts. A siren would sound, often in the middle of the night, and my dad would head to his squadron where they might scramble the jets he flew. Unbeknownst to me his jet was armed with nuclear warheads. In a real threat he would fly away and we could have been the target of enemies.

Who could name all of those who were enemy to one another? Although almost every child remembers some enemy, name calling bullies, physical bullies, or vindictive individuals. I had three: Diana, Terry and Wanda. January 1958, I was the new girl in class and Diana told all the girls not to be my friend. It was a lonely year. I was later told about Diana's decree. What motivated her? I'll never know. Terry on the other hand visited my house with other girls, stole my diary and wounded me deeply. She took away my ability to trust girls my age at school, and my ability to write freely in my journal. Wanda thought I lacked school spirit, she was going to beat it into me. She did not succeed; the bus driver grabbed her by the collar, even if he hadn't done so she would have failed.

Our worst enemies aren't school bullies or people of other countries. The media can turn people into a threatening "they," hence our own government's internment of Japanese in World War II. We need to be concerned when a segment of society is maligned, and fight fear mongering.

We come back to the word fear. It's at the root and stem of worldwide problems, and even worse, in ourselves. Driven by fear the outcomes aren't positive. Walt Kelly was right: "We have met the enemy and he is us."

GONE

The bone white snag above Beaver Creek fell
down in a storm. It was a two-tined fork pointed
skyward, a favored perch of magpies, its alabaster
brightness a cynosure obscured the trees beside it.

It began to lean after heavy spring rains saturated
the ground, we thought it might take down a tree
beside it but instead sheared off only a few limbs.

Now the space it occupied appears gap-toothed,
and gone forever is its sculptural beauty—that fork
tuning the wind—will be missed until memory
of it fades and what is not there is what is there.

ACKNOWLEDGMENTS

With thanks to the writers around the table at Bellingham's Independent Writers' Studio and to the Confluence Poets.

"Grandma Nelle," *Clover, A Literary Rag*, V. 4 2012. p. 8.

"Thanksgiving," *Talk*, a chapbook created for Western Washington University staff show. June 1998. p.10.

"Fish in Our Albums," Methow Arts Alliance, Summer 2013. p.13.

"White Fence," *Clover, A Literary Rag*, V. 5, 2013. Included in exhibit *Visions of Verse*, Winter 2014 Confluence Gallery and the chapbook/catalogue of show. p. 25.

"Traces of Christie," *Clover, A Literary Rag* V. 12, 2016. p. 27

"Our Mother's Laundry," *Clover, A Literary Rag*, V. 9, 2015. p. 29.

"For Dana Irish," *Talk*, a chapbook created for Western Washington University staff show. June 1998. p. 31.

"Dysart Reunion," *Talk*, a chapbook created for Western Washington University staff show. June 1998. p. 35.

"Moving Days," *Clover, A Literary Rag*, V. 9, 2015. p. 37.

"Korean War Memories," *Clover, A Literary Rag*, V. 10., 2015 p. 39.

"My Mother's Wishes," *Clover, A Literary Rag, V 7*. p. 43.

"The Royal Hudson," *Clover, A Literary Rag*, V. 4, 2012. p. 47.

"Normandy, Day 1," poem shown as broadside with photography by Jack Kienast for Blue Horse Gallery in Bellingham, WA. July 2010. p. 49.

"Mercredi 13 Mai 2009," poem shown as broadside with photography by Jack Kienast for Blue Horse Gallery in Bellingham, WA. July 2010. p. 51.

"La Parisienne," poem shown as broadside with photography by Jack Kienast for Blue Horse Gallery in Bellingham, WA. July 2010. p. 53.

"The Seine," poem shown as broadside with photography by Jack Kienast for Blue Horse Gallery in Bellingham, WA. July 2010. p. 54.

"Nora," *Talk*, a chapbook created for Western Washington University staff show. June1998. p. 55.

"Traveling with Edna St. Vincent Millay," *Clover, A Literary Rag*, V.1, 2010. p. 57.

"Cordial with Ms. Crow" *Noisy Water: Poetry from Whatcom County, Washington*, Edited by Luther Allen and J. L. Kleinberg 2015. p. 61.

"Jake," *Clover, A Literary Rag*, V. 2, 2011. p. 63.

"Howl," *Clover, A Literary Rag*, V. 1, 2010. p. 64.

"Construction Dogs," *Clover, A Literary Rag*, V. 6, 2013. p. 65.

"December Snow," *Clover, A Literary Rag*, V. 4, 2012. p. 68.

"Watching the Storm," Sue C. Boynton Poetry Contest Merit award winner. Whatcom County Washington 2009. Reprinted in *Poetry Walk, Sue C. Boynton, The First Five Years 2006-2010*. p. 67.

"Witness to Winter Sailings," *Clover, A Literary Rag*, V.10, 2015. p. 69.

"Port of Bellingham," *Windfall: A Journal of p.etry of p.ace*, Fall 2012. p. 70.

"Saturday Morning ...," *Clover, A Literary Rag*, V. 3, 2012, p. 72.

"Eastern Washington, the Palouse," *Clover, A Literary Rag*, V. 3, 2012. p. 75.

"Life Cycles in the Methow," *Clover, A Literary Rag*, V. 8, 2014. p. 77.

"Feast," *Clover, A Literary Rag*, V. 5, 2013. p. 79.

"Snowplow Sidewalks," *Clover, A Literary Rag*, V. 12, 2016. p. 81.

"Pine Trees . . .," *Clover, A Literary Rag,* V. 6, 2013. p. 82.

"In Envy of Ravens," *Clover, A Literary Rag,* V. 2, 2011. p. 83.

"Summer Storm, 2013," *Windfall: A Journal of Poetry of Place* Spring 2014. p. 85.

"Above Onion Creek," *Clover, A Literary Rag,* V. 3, 2012. p. 87.

"News from the Methow . . .," Included in "The Methow Valley's Summer of Disaster," a supplement to the *Methow Valley News,* December 2014. p. 88.

"Her Final Wishes," *Clover, A Literary Rag,* V. 13, 2017.

"Parents," *Clover, A Literary Rag,* V. 12, 2016. p.107.

"Lost & Found," *Clover, A Literary Rag,* V. 9, 2015. p. 109.

"December Visit to Greenacres," *Clover, A Literary Rag,* V. 4, 2012. p. 111.

"Grief," *Clover, A Literary Rag,* V. 11, 2016. p. 113.

"Esther Maria (Anderson) Keepers," *Talk,* a chapbook created for Western Washington University staff show. June 1998. p. 114.

"Calculating Deaths..." *Clover A Literary Rag,* V. 7, 2014. p. 116.

"Gravity," *Clover, A Literary Rag,* V. 7, 2014. p. 118.

"Certitude," *Clover, A Literary Rag,* V. 6, 2013. p. 119.

"I am a Vessel," *Clover, A Literary Rag* V. 8, 2014. p. 120.

"Update," *Clover A Literary Rag,* V. 13, 2017.

"Aching," *Clover A Literary Rag,* V. 2, 2011. p. 127.

"Desire," *Clover, A Literary Rag,* V. 5, 2013. p. 129.

"To Sin by Silence," poem shown as broadside with photography by Jack Kienast for Blue Horse Gallery in Bellingham, WA. July 2010. p. 130.

"Enemies," *Whatcom Writes! One Book Together,* Borderline Press, Bellingham, WA, 2012. p. 136.

"Gone," *Clover, A Literary Rag,* V. 13, 2017. p. 85.

www.ingramcontent.com/pod-product-compliance
Lightning Source LLC
Chambersburg PA
CBHW022010090426
42741CB00007B/968